A Sesame Street Toddler Book

I Have to Go

Featuring Jim Henson's Sesame Street Muppets

By Anna Ross • Illustrated by Norman Gorbaty

Random House / Children's Television Workshop

Library of Congress Cataloging-in-Publication Data:
Ross, Anna. I have to go : featuring Jim Henson's Sesame Street Muppets / by Anna Ross ; illustrated by Norman Gorbaty.   p.   cm.–
(A Sesame Street toddler book) SUMMARY: Little Grover goes to the bathroom all by himself. ISBN: 0-394-86051-9   [1. Toilet training–Fiction.
2. Puppets–Fiction] I. Gorbaty, Norman, ill. II. Title. III. Series. PZ7.R71962Iah   1990   [E]–dc 20   89-34542

Manufactured in Italy   8 9 10

Little Grover was riding his
choo-choo.

"Chug-chug-chug."

Suddenly he pulled down hard
on the air brake.

"Chuff-chuff-hisssss." He came
to a stop.

"I have to go," said Little Grover.

Little Big Bird was pounding pegs when Little Grover went by. "Hey, Grover," said Little Big Bird. "Want to hammer?"

"No, thank you," said
Little Grover. "I have to go."
"Go where?" Little
Big Bird wondered.

Little Ernie and Little Bert were having a tea party when Little Grover went by.

"Do you want some tea?" asked Little Ernie.

"No tea for me," said Little Grover. "I have to go."

"Go where?" asked Little Ernie.

Little Cookie Monster was mixing batter when Little Grover went by.

"Look, Grover!" Cookie Monster cried. "Want to make cookies?"

"No time now," said Little Grover.
"I have to go."

"Me too?" Little Cookie Monster
asked. But Little Grover was gone.

Little Betty Lou rang her cash register. "Do you want to play store, Little Grover?"

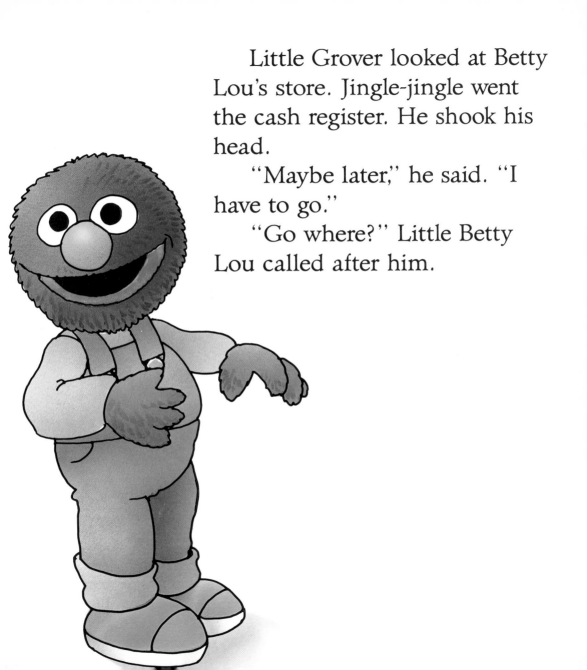

Little Grover looked at Betty
Lou's store. Jingle-jingle went
the cash register. He shook his
head.

"Maybe later," he said. "I
have to go."

"Go where?" Little Betty
Lou called after him.

"I have to find Mommy," said Little Grover. "And there she is right now." Little Grover's mommy was in the garden watering the flowers.

"Want to help, Little Grover?"

"No, thank you. Guess what,
Mommy!" he said.

"What, Little Grover?"

"I have to go!"

"You do, Little Grover?" said his mommy. She put down her watering can and stood up. "Oh, my goodness. Come inside!"

Little Grover followed his mommy into the bathroom.

There was his very own little potty.

Grover's mommy unfastened his straps.

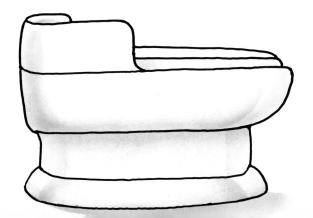

And Little Grover
went. All by himself.

Then his mommy
fastened his straps.

"You are getting so big, Little Grover," said his mommy. "And I am very proud of you."